The Theatre of
STEVEN BERKOFF

1. Sydney, Australia (1982). *The Fall of the House of Usher* – getting ready.

2 (*overleaf*). Steven Berkoff languidly seated as Herod. Carmen Du Sautoy ever watchful as Herodias while the 'Executioner', Peter Brennan, awaits instructions in the Royal National Theatre production of Oscar Wilde's *Salome* (1989).

The Theatre of Steven Berkoff

Text by
Steven Berkoff

Photographs by
Roger Morton, Martha Swope, Nobby Clark

Christopher Pearce, Lore Bermbach, Jaacov Agor, Robert McFarlane

**John Haynes, Alastair Muir, Neil Libbert, Cordelia Weedon,
Christopher Casler, Wilfried Hösl, Robert Pederson**

Methuen Drama

METHUEN DRAMA

First published in Great Britain in 1992
by Methuen Drama

Grateful acknowledgement is made to reprint extracts from the
following copyright material:
Metamorphosis © Steven Berkoff 1981, 1988, Amber Lane Press
The Trial © Steven Berkoff 1981, 1988, Amber Lane Press
The Fall of the House of Usher © Steven Berkoff 1977, 1990,
Amber Lane Press
Agamemnon © 1977, 1990, Amber Lane Press
Decadence © Steven Berkoff 1981, 1982, 1983, 1986, 1989, Faber
and Faber
East © Steven Berkoff 1977, 1978, 1982, 1989, Faber and Faber
West © Steven Berkoff 1985, 1989, Faber and Faber
Greek © 1980, 1982, 1983, 1986, 1989, Faber and Faber
Kvetch © Steven Berkoff 1986, Faber and Faber
Sink the Belgrano © Steven Berkoff 1987, Faber and Faber
Introduction to *Salome* © Steven Berkoff 1989, Faber and Faber
I Am Hamlet © Steven Berkoff 1989, Faber and Faber

A CIP catalogue record for this title
is available from the British Library

ISBN 0 413 67340 5

Photoset by Rowland Phototypesetting Ltd,
Bury St Edmunds, Suffolk

I dedicate this book
to my fellow actors
and musicians who
participated in all
the following productions.

Metamorphosis
at The Round House (1969)
Jeannie James
George Little
Petra Markham
Christopher Munke

Metamorphosis
at The Mermaid (1986)
Linda Marlowe
Garry Olsen
Saskia Reeves
Tim Roth
Music: Mark Glentworth

Metamorphosis
in Düsseldorf (1983)
Biggi Fischer
Christianne Gott
Karlheinz Vietsch
Michael Prelle
Bernd Jeschek

Metamorphosis
in New York (1989)
Rene Aubergenois
Mikhail Baryshnikov
Laura Esterman
Mitch Kreindell
T J Meyer
Madeleine Potter
Music: Larry Spivac

The Trial
at The Round House (1973)
Judith Alderson
Teresa Dabreu
Wolf Kahler
Hilton McRae
Terry McGinity
Linda Marlowe
Alfredo Michelson
Barry Philips
Barry Stanton
Bill Stewart

The Trial
in Düsseldorf (1976)
Udo Bodnick
Helmut Everke
Suzanne Geyer
Jutta Hahn
Bernt Heinzelmann
Peter Hommen
Barbara Khol
Rene Ramser
Hans Christian Rudolph
Gisbert Ruschkamp
Brita Sommer
Edgar Sommer
Edgar Walther
Music: Peter Schmidt

House of Usher
in London (1975)
Shelley Lee
Alfredo Michelson
Terry McGinity
Music: David Ellis

House of Usher
in Australia (1982)
Terry McGinity
Anne Stainer
Music: John Prior

Agamemnon
at Greenwich (1976)
Lawrence Held
Wolf Kahler
Shelley Lee
Hilton McRae
Terry McGinity
Day Murch
Deborah Norton
Anna Nygh
Barry Philips
Matthew Scurfield
Music: David Toop
Paul Burwell

Agamemnon
in Haifa (1979)
Aharon Almog
Te'Hia Danon
Suhil Haddad
Makram Khpouri
Amos Lavi
Shabtai Konorty
Avinoam Mor-Haim
Dani Muggia
Joanna Peled
Zvi Serper
Asher SarFaty
Shmuel Wolf
Zeev Shimshoni
Music: Zohar Levy

Agamemnon
in Los Angeles (1984)
Christine Avila
Dewayne Brady
Arthur Burghardt
Jessie Ferguson
John Lafayette
Stuart Mabray
Raymond Oliver
Roger Guenveur Smith
Diane Sommerfield
Le Tari
Darin Taylor

Hamlet
in London (1980)
David Auker
Sally Bentley
Rory Edwards
Bob Hornery
Wolf Kahler
Linda Marlowe
Terry McGinity
David Meyer
Tony Meyer
Barry Philips
Chloë Salaman
Matthew Scurfield
Gary Whelan
Nigel Williams
Music: John Prior

Coriolanus
in New York (1989)
Ethan T Bowen
André Braugher
Larry Bryggman
Deryl Caitlyn
Ashley Crow
Keith David
Albert Farrar
Moses Gunn
Paul Hecht
Thomas Kopache
Tom McGowan
Joseph C Phillips
Armand Schultz
Roger Guenveur Smith
Matt Sullivan
John Towey
Christopher Walken
Sharon Washington
Irene Worth
Music: Larry Spivac

Coriolanus
in Munich (1991)
Rufus Beck
Hans Stetter
Raidar Müller-Elmau
Rudolf Donath
Georg Weber
Bernhard Baier
Hans Piesbergen
Michael Vogtmann
Lola Müthel
Sona MacDonald
Christiane Roßbach
Achim Barrenstein
Wolfgang Bauer
Bernhard Bettermann
Thomas Kylau
Hans-Werner Meyer
Nik Neureiter
Hans Piesbergen
Wolfram Rupperti
Georg Weber
Hans Habryka
Franco Lauria

East
in London (1976)
David Delve
Anna Nygh
Barry Philips
Matthew Scurfield
Music: Neil Hansford

Greek
in London (1980)
Linda Marlowe
Deirdre Morris
Barry Philips
Matthew Scurfield

Greek
in London (1988)
Georgia Brown
Gillian Eaton
Bruce Payne

West
in London (1983)
Ralph Brown
Steve Dixon
Rory Edwards
Susan Kyd
John Joyce
Bruce Payne
Ken Sharrock
Stella Tanner
Garry Freer
Music: Mark Glentworth

Kvetch
in London (1991)
Anita Dobson
Henry Goodman
Thelma Ruby
Stanley Lebor

Sink the Belgrano
in London (1986)
Tam Dean Burn
George Dillon
Richard Earthy
Rory Edwards
Louise Gold
Eugene Lipinski
Terry McGinity
Barry Stanton
Bill Stewart
Maggie Steed
Edward Tudor-Pole

Salome
in London (1986)
Peter Brennan
Jason Carter
Katrin Cartlidge
Imogen Claire
George Dillon
Rory Edwards
Wolf Kahler
Maria Pastel
Tim Potter
Vincenzo Ricotta
Carmen Du Sautoy
Katherine Schlesinger
Pianist: Eleanor Alberga

CONTENTS

The following photographs represent the images from just over twenty years of work as a director in the theatre.

Those decades have been most kind to me since they straddled momentous changes in the arts from the liberation of the theatre from its realistic stance in the Sixties to a more conservative and watchful eye during the Eighties – to what now in the Nineties? The late Sixties was a time of unshackling and abandonment to the joys of Dionysus and the exploration of the senses. The well-made play with its limited confines and its stressed and forced dialogues had no magic for the new apostles of the theatre. I was tutored by the blazing experiments of the early Living Theatre that came over from America under the inspired direction of Julian Beck. At the Mermaid Theatre I was privileged to watch them at work in *The Brig*, a production which has stayed in my mind ever since as a great piece of drama should. I saw that text, sound and gesture could create the cruellest and most powerful theatrical scenario even when based on a realistic theme.

During the Sixties I was also privileged to be able to study mime in Paris with the talented teacher Claude Chagrin and then with her master Jacques le Coq. His techniques gave me the opportunity to invent ways of presenting works whereby all elements of the human being are brought into motion. Some call it 'total theatre' and nowadays 'physical theatre'.

Many of the works shown here were seeded by the cross-fertilization of the many influences that were then prevalent. It was a fruitful time and the proliferation of theatre groups was no less astounding than the fact that the theatre seemed to want to claw back its ritualistic origins. Ritual is characterised by its concern with human involvement and the sharing of ideas. Egos were considered vapid stuff and human and natural forces were the primary objective in these kinds of drama. Archetypal subjects more relevant to Jung than Shaftsbury Avenue were being used as source material. Groups evolved that were interested in trying to express bold ideas; I remember titles of works like *Beowulf, Antigone, Frankenstein* and *Genesis* then being the contemporary crop.

So naturally I gravitated to Kafka, Poe, even the heady Aeschylus, given to me as a benefit for having had the opportunity to direct it at RADA. In each instance I decided to eventually write my own versions of drama. Why not! I revelled in the primal emotions and classic

INTRODUCTION

3. Berkoff as Hamlet – *'To be or not to be'* –
I devised so many ways of performing this speech
but in the end made it as simple and direct as I could.

tragedy that might make for a theatre directed at the audience's senses as well as their minds. The non-human and spiritual fascinated me as much as the human. The beetle in Kafka's *Metamorphosis* is as cogent and vital an alienated being as is Jimmy Porter in *Look Back in Anger*, the added advantage being that you had to create a man plus an insect.

My own attempts at writing naturally were affected by this surge of creative energy that, like a flood-tide, was creeping into every tiny tributary of theatrical activity. I attempted to write plays whose themes were non-representational images of human behaviour rather than simply life-like 'characters' – *East* emerged in 1975 followed by *West* in 1977 followed by *Greek* in 1980, all of which could not have been written had I not been stimulated by the idea of a theatre drawing on its ancient myths. *Decadence* followed these and then the others you see here.

I was lucky to have seen the dawning of the Age of Aquarius and then its demise. I was fortunate to see the works of the French performer and director Jean-Louis Barrault and the American experimentalists Joe Chaikin and Tom O'Horgan. Who can ever forget O'Horgan's production of *Futz* at the small Mercury Theatre. For individual power I could sit at the feet of the great thespian master, Laurence Olivier. For yearly sabbaticals I had Peter Daubeny's World Theatre Season at the Aldwych Theatre to look forward to. I witnessed Peter Brook's summit of creativity in *Marat/Sade* and *A Midsummer Night's Dream*. At the Old Vic Theatre I saw the Berliner Ensemble do dynamically physical productions of Brecht's *Arturo Ui* and *Coriolanus*. In a word I was 'fortunate'. I saw the cycle of great artists reach a peak and was there to catch it as it happened.

If I can say I was influenced, I hope I can also say that I absorbed the best and mixed it with my own experience. In the end one has to carry the waves forward and in some ways be responsible for the baton until one must pass it on. We are all carriers of traditions and, like an exercise, we change the information given to us in turn by adding our own input.

Nothing can capture essential theatrical moments – and in some strange way immortalise them forever – as a still black and white photograph taken by a shrewd and selective artistic eye. Sometimes after a production has closed or when I am reconstructing a revival Phoenix-like out of the ashes of memory, I will browse through these pictures to restore in my mind's eye the moments, the sound and the fury of the action. Most were taken in the midst of the heat of performances. I often find here images I had never imagined creating and would be instantly moved by seeing the sheer exertion of actors exposed in that struggle of supreme effort.

I am rather proud of this collection of selected prints. They carefully express not just the style of my direction but a surging physicality and energy in my various ensemble of players. So I am indebted to the men and women whose pictures are represented here. First on the list of insightful photographers I have had the good fortune to collaborate with over twenty-plus years is Roger Morton, who I worked with from the beginning when I first staged Kafka's *The Trial* in London at the Round House, Chalk Farm, in 1973. Thereafter Roger Morton photographed several of our works and was our recorder for nearly ten years. Almost half of this book shows his work. To him I am truly grateful for his friendship and moral support. I must also pay homage to other photographers whose meticulous work brought to life in black and white: *Agamemnon* in Israel, where the tide of fleshy conflict in war is tersely caught by Jaacov Agor; *The Trial* at the Düsseldorf Schauspielhaus, where I received an extraordinary collection of that play and of *Metamorphosis* by Lore Bermbach; my own play *East*, shot during a 1978 performance in a hot airless theatre in Sydney, Australia, by Robert McFarlane, giving me a fresh impression of that work. He also is represented here by *The Fall of the House of Usher*. After many productions around the world of my own adaptation of Kafka's *Metamorphosis*, I must thank New York photographer Martha Swope who so brilliantly caught the kinetic quality of the performance and the tension in the action in ways I have never before witnessed in this play. A host of other extraordinary photographers are also represented here with specific key photographs: Christopher Pearce's portfolio of my plays *Decadence* and *West*, Chris Casler's study of the all-Black Los Angeles production of *Agamemnon*, John Haynes's expressive view of *Sink the Belgrano*, plus magnificent isolated shots by Cordelia Weedon, Neil Libbert, Alastair Muir and Wilfried Hösl. Lastly, I cannot think of a time when a photographer imbued me with confidence in quite the same way as did Nobby Clark's haunting study of *Salome*. After looking at what Nobby saw through the lens of his camera, I felt his photos captured all the elusive moods of that production and are probably more akin to paintings.

Finally, I must thank: Liz Cook for her initial enthusiasm and help in formatting this book, my agent Joanna Marston for her unstinting support over the years and . . . Clara.

Steven Berkoff
London 1991

METAMORPHOSIS

I came to Kafka on reading *Metamorphosis*. I saw in him the most marvellous exertions of the imagination working inside the desperation of a strangled soul, this frightened human being – and thereby releasing its horrors. He touched me in all my chords of being from grotesque to simple, sublime humanity. No other writer quite manages this with the same power and insight.

A skeletal framework of steel scaffolding suggesting an abstract sculpture of a giant insect is stretched across the stage – this serves as a home of the family or carapace. The stage is void of all props – everything is mimed – apart from three black stools (metal) situated equidistant downstage for the family to use. The scaffolding narrows at the back, containing in its centre Gregor's room or cage. He is on a small ramp (2' 6") suggesting always that Gregor is hovering above the family. He is always watching – forever aware. The living quarters that the family use are demarcated by sharply lit areas, thus when Greta opens Gregor's door a hard light snaps down on the cage indicating the family can now see him. When this light is off the door is shut – that is stage reality for the family – the second reality for the audience is, of course, that he is always seen in half light but his family cannot see him. Within his cage are horizontal metal bars allowing Gregor to crawl gradually up the wall. At the top of the cage the bars fan out to the edge of the scaffolding downstage to enable Gregor at a later point of the play to climb along the ceiling upside down and beetle-like.

Since Gregor's beetle metamorphosis is an attitude deliberately taken to expressively show his inner-state, his naked dehumanized personality, a struggling insect, I chose to adapt and direct the play as formally as possible, suggesting the family's joy and anguish very often in fixed attitudes – choreographed reactions – Victorian gestures, frozen movement reminiscent of old prints. The movement becomes an analogue to the hard, bright, mechanical insect movement of Gregor – they might be separate units of the beetle themselves. This style, rather than diminishing the impact of the story by reducing naturalistic stage activity, did for many have an even more powerful effect, as if the memory of events and of people is retained in the mind's eye almost as stills – sometimes slightly blurred and out of focus. Perhaps this is why 'old photographs' strike so powerfully chords of association.

4. Gregor Samsa keeps on his father's back, as if he wants to hurt him, but Mr Samsa has no trouble pulling Gregor's feeble limbs away from his throat. The New York production with Mikhail Baryshnikov as Gregor and Rene Aubergenois as Mr Samsa.

5. *'I liked hanging from the ceiling, it was better than the floor, one breathed more easily.'* Meanwhile Gregor's family decide to empty his room. Petra Markham as Greta, Jeannie James as Mrs Samsa and Berkoff as the gymnastic bug. Here and opposite the 1969 Round House production.

6. *'As Gregor Samsa awoke one morning from a night of uneasy dreams he found himself transformed into a gigantic insect.'*

7. *'I can hear you, you think I can't understand you simply because you can't understand me.*

8. *'I'll put my clothes on at once, pack my samples and be off.'*

9. *'Sounds like something fell in the next room?'* Berkoff as the oppressed Mr Samsa and Garry Olsen as the Chief Clerk.

10. *'Apple for you Gregor!'* Mr Samsa hurls a mimed apple at the prostrate bug played by Tim Roth. The Mermaid Theatre, London, production 1986.

11–15 (*left*). Tim Roth explores his environment designed by Martin Beaton and Berkoff.

16.

GREGOR: *Gregor was quite unpracticed in moving backward.*

MR SAMSA: *His father for his part wanted him out of the room as soon as possible.*

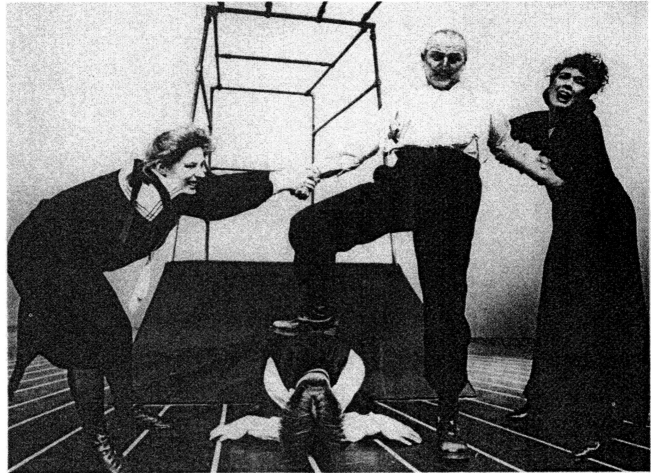

19. Gregor watches as Mrs Samsa and Greta plan to empty his room. He is about to leap into the room. The 1983 Düsseldorf production here and the next four pages.

17 & 18. Linda Marlowe as Mrs Samsa and Saskia Reeves as Greta attempt to pull the enraged Mr Samsa (Berkoff) away from Gregor (Tim Roth).

20. The family all listen outside the imagined door for Gregor to answer. Gregor attempts to turn the 'key' to open the door.

21 & 22.

GREGOR: *They want to turn my room into a naked den for some beast to roam in.*

GRETA: *I want to shift some furniture so that he can move around more easily.*

MOTHER: *It's so heavy. You'll never manage it alone.*

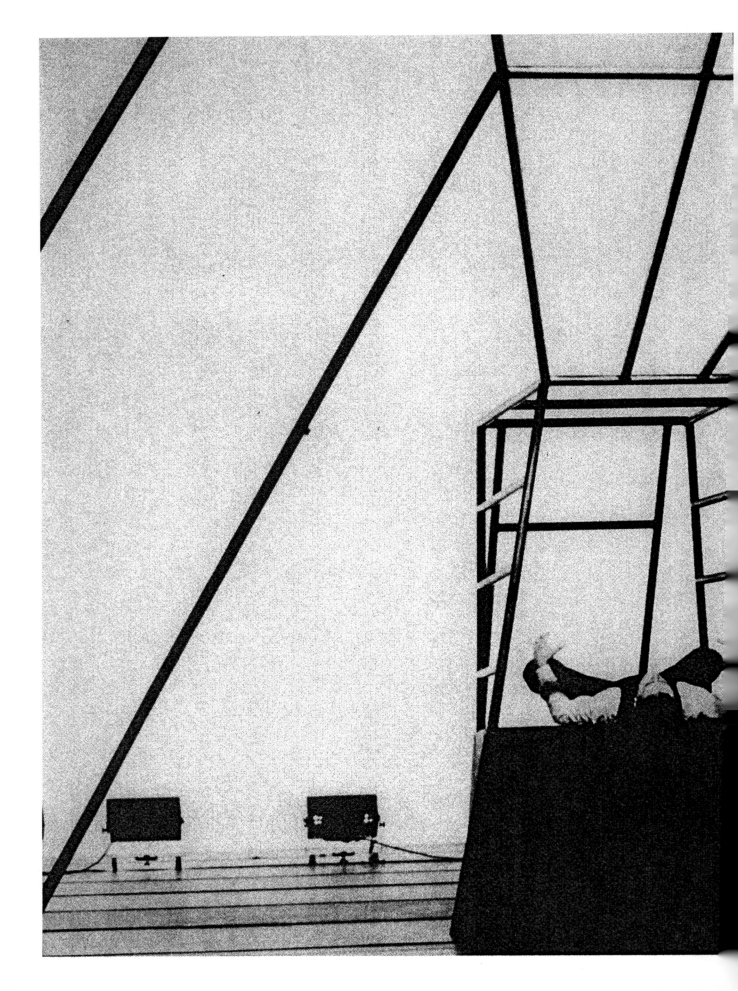

23 (previous pages).
The death of Gregor.

MRS SAMSA: *The crocuses will just
be coming out.*

24. Misha Baryshnikov – our final beetle
in the 1989 New York Broadway production.

GREGOR: *I like hanging from the ceiling – it's better
than the floor – one breathes more easily . . .*

25 & 26.
Misha explores his
environment and feels
quite at home.

27. Family and Chief Clerk are
most perturbed that Gregor is not
at work.
From left: Madeleine Potter, Laura
Esterman, Misha, Rene Aubergenois
(the Family) and Mitch Kreindell (the
Chief Clerk).

28. Gregor eventually reveals himself to the suitably horrified expressions of the Family. Yet in the nightmare world life must go on.

GREGOR: *I'll put my clothes on at once, pack my samples and be off, I want to work you see . . .*

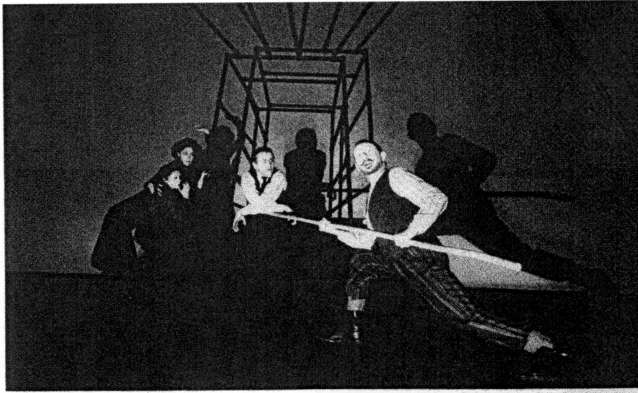

29. Rene Aubergenois pushes
Gregor back into his room. Misha
doesn't look too pleased.

30. A particularly interesting photo
showing each member of the family
in a physical attitude that reflects the
core of the action.

MR SAMSA: *Apple for you*
Gregor.
MRS SAMSA: *Climb Gregor, climb*
the walls, you can
climb.
GRETA: *Escape, Gregor,*
escape.

31.

GREGOR: *What a quiet life our family has been leading.*

32 (following pages). Gregor stares out of the window. A striking image caught by a combination of accident, shadow and light.

GREGOR: *Everything is grey, everything.*

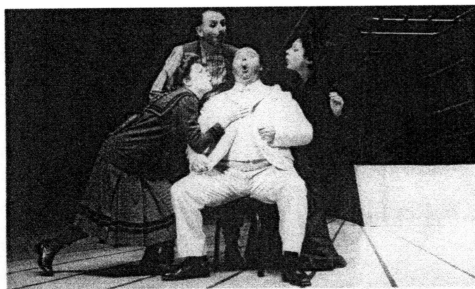

33. The Lodger is played with great enthusiasm and comic energy by T J Meyer.

LODGER: *Oooh! The potatoes are hot.*

The Family obligingly cools them.

34. Misha in pre-insect state.

GREGOR: *I'm Gregor Samsa. This is my sister Greta.*
GRETA: *This is my brother Gregor.*

35. This photo expressively captures the web that traps the entire Family. They are listening to Gregor 'moving about' in his room. Like three spiders they react to every sound, every movement, while Gregor is perfectly attuned to his 'insect' state.

What is K's, alias Kafka's, guilt? Nothing so complex as world guilt or messianic martyrdom. But K's guilt, for which he must die, is the guilt of betrayal: the guilt of betraying his inner spirit to the safety of mediocrity. For every action that is not expressed through fear, for every desire that wells up in the breast and is not given vent in action through fear turns into a little rat of guilt that gnaws away at your vitals. For every shout held back, for every venture not ventured on, for every regret in the soul, for every compromise you make and slur you took adds to the sorry storehouse of guilt that screams out for justice. The soul screams out for vengeance, starved as it is in its dark and stinking hovel. Guilt is the difference between what your spirit sings out for and what your courage permits you to take. Joseph K's guilt – Kafka's guilt.

'Before the door stands the doorkeeper' is the opening line of the parable related to K by the priest from whom he seeks salvation; and a man is waiting there to gain admission to the Law. The doorkeeper cannot admit him just yet and thus begins the ludicrous parable investigating every contingency and nuance of the Law. An exegesis of vacillation. The man waits for years and years but did not thrust himself through because he believed the doorkeeper when he said that there were other doors and each man guarding them was successively stronger than he. Burst through the doors. But the Law demands due process and one must wait. But in the end he dies of waiting, when the door to the Law was meant only for him. You cannot wait for what is due to you. You must seize it.

We devised a door. A wooden rectangular frame that stood by itself. In later productions they became steel. Ten frames became the set. The set became the environment. A set should be able to melt in an instant and never represent a real heavy piece of pseudo-reality. So much waste. Our set of ten screens became the story and as the story could move from moment to moment so could our set—no long waits for a scene change but as a flash with the magician's sleight of hand. We could be even quicker than the story. A room could become a trap, a prison, expand and contract and even spin around the protagonist Joseph K. This enabled us to recreate the environment – both physical and mental – of the book.

THE TRIAL

36. Bill Stewart as Joseph K in the 1973 Round House production.

K: *I'm an accused man like all of you. I only want to know the date of my interrogation.*

37. Antony Sher, as the Bank Clerk Joseph K, and a leering Berkoff, as the surrealist Court Painter Titorelli, share a moment in the frame during the 1991 Royal National Theatre production.

TITORELLI: *But my paintings are very good.*
K: *I don't want your paintings, I'd rather die!*

38. Bill Stewart and Chorus of the accusers.

39. Two Guards (Wolf Kahler and Barry Philips) search the room of Joseph K. The Chorus wait behind their doors watching this invasion of privacy.

40.
GUARD 1:   *A lovely coat . . . I'll try it on . . . How do I look?*
GUARD 2:   *Beautiful!*

41.
GUARD 1:   *Where are your papers?*
GUARD 2:   *Search him.*

42.

GUARD 1:   *We are your friendly warders who stand closer to you than anyone else right now.*

GUARD 2:   *We're just humble subordinates who can scarcely find our way through a legal document.*

43.

GUARD 1:   *Did you hear that Frank? He doesn't know the law yet he claims to be innocent.*

GUARD 2:   *You'll never make a man like that see reason.*

44.

JOSEPH K: *It might be a joke concocted by my colleague for my 30th birthday . . . Now if I laugh, they'll probably laugh with me.*

45.
ACCUSED: *Some of us have been waiting for years.*

46 (opposite).
GUARD: *We're going to be flogged because you denounced us!*

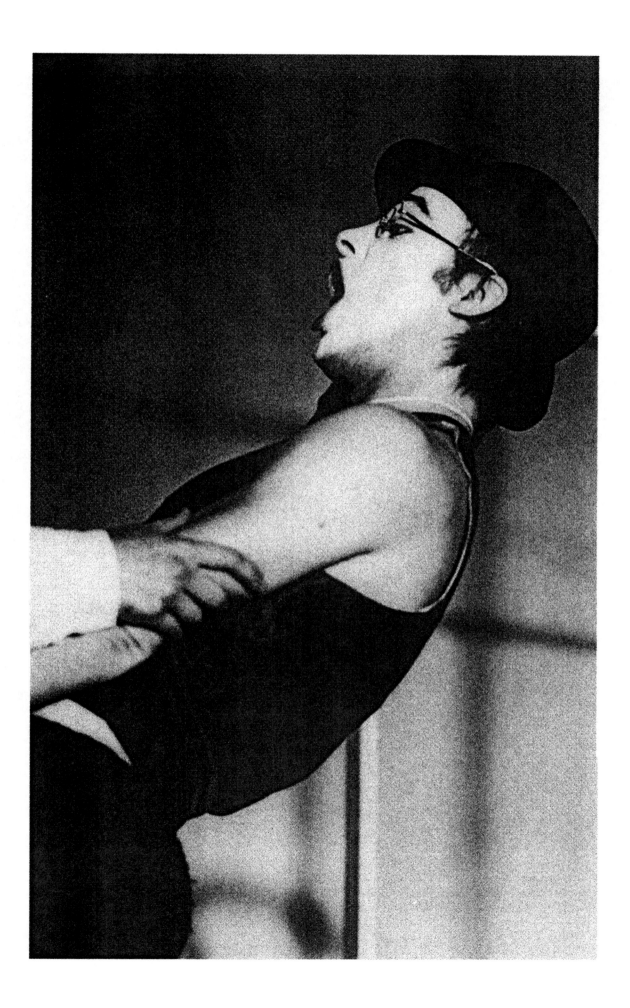

47. The corridor of the lawcourt seems to dissolve as
Joseph K is trapped within. The frames form a multi-purpose
mobile 'set' that change shape instantly to become doors,
rooms, corridors, windows and mirrors.

48. Joseph K trying to find his way out of the labyrinthian 'corridors' of the lawcourt. He feels he's been framed.

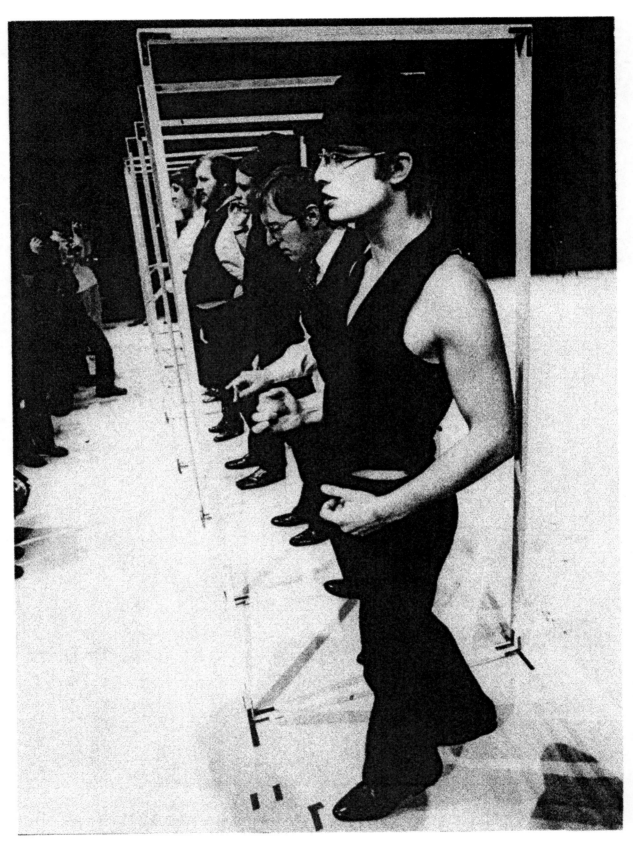

49. The long office. Joseph K assumes his position at the
bank.

TYPISTS: *Good morning, Mr K.*

50. Inside the Cathedral. Alfredo Michelson as the Priest.

PRIEST: *I am here for you. I am the prison chaplain . . . I had you summoned here to talk to you.*

51. The Priest stands in what is really a suspended version of the frames. The 1976 Düsseldorf Schauspielhaus production. We found that linear shape dominated all our structures.

PRIEST: *The verdict is not suddenly arrived at. The proceedings gradually merge into the verdict. What is your next move?*

K: *There are several possibilities I haven't explored yet.*

52. Huld the lawyer surrounded by his 'clients', who live in the same house and who are too afraid to leave lest changes should occur in their case.

HULD: *To be frank with you, I know why you came. Your case is far too interesting to refuse to take it on. I accept the challenge.*

K: *I don't understand. How can you know?*

53 (left). Joseph K (centre) in the office, the proud assistant manager.

54 & 55 (bottom left and right). Joseph K entering the cathedral.

56 (below). Joseph K tries to stop the frenzied activity in the corridor of the waiting Accused.

57. Joseph K enters the corridor. He becomes dizzy and the walls seem to sway. The wooden frames we used in the Round House production have now turned to polished steel in Düsseldorf. This is one of the most amazing pictures that any photographer has captured of my productions of *The Trial*.

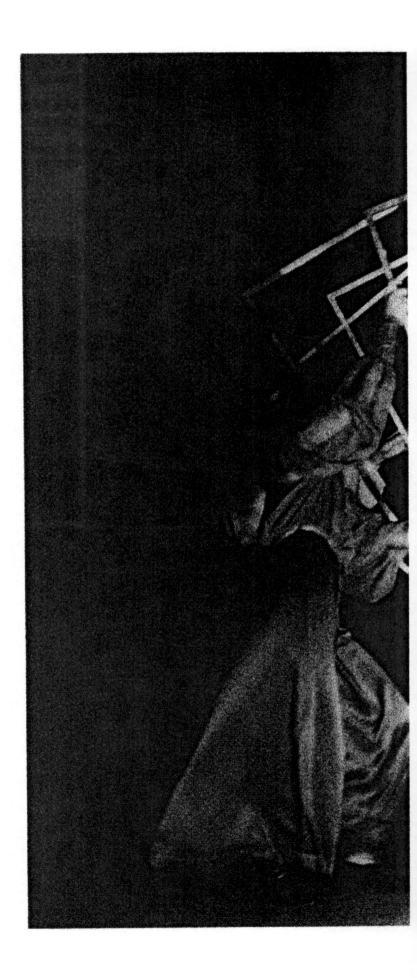

58. The rope that was once his escape route is now his executioner. Joseph K took what he thought was the safe route but got caught in the snare. End of play.

K: *Wait! There must be some arguments in my favour that have been overlooked. Wait! Where is my Judge whom I have never seen . . . Will someone help me? I hold out my hands . . .*

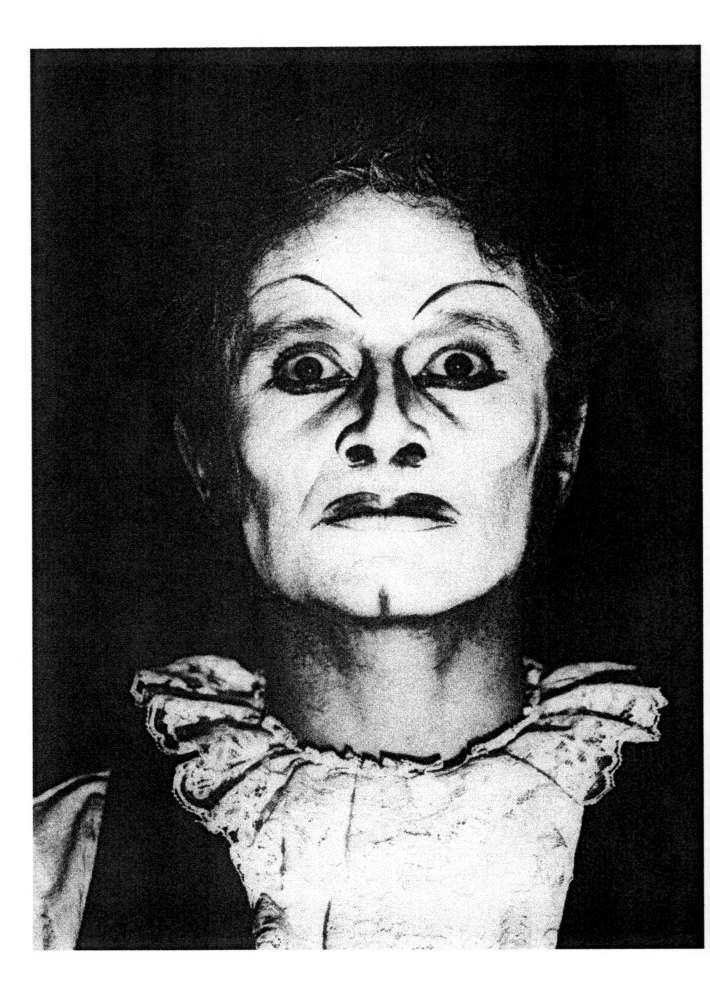

THE FALL OF THE HOUSE OF USHER

When this play works one lives on the crest of a wave when all elements fuse into a dynamic whole of music, light, shape and words. Then one is transported to another world as an actor and, I hope, as an audience . . .

To dwell within the world of Poe is to commit oneself to the self-imposed exile of the anchorite. To enter into this confinement of senses painfully attenuated to vibrate to the slightest tremor of the outside or inside world is to discover the spirituality of Poe via his chorus, Roderick Usher. But since one is affected by this journey one may at the same time chart the spirituality within oneself. This exile demands constant fidelity; the playing of Roderick Usher's arabesque fantasies each night permits no cheating and coruscates the days in a gentle wash of acid. All is dominated by the evening. All excesses are curbed . . . The temperament hones to the delicate knife-edged sensitivity of Usher . . . whose senses 'are painfully acute'.

To play him is to know him. One cannot approach such a life as Usher's without absorbing his texture, by the quivering nature of a person who is all nerve endings . . . not so abnormal but wholly aware to the degree where life is no longer tolerable, where it can only be made tolerable by the deliberate blunting of the senses. This he is unprepared to do, necessary as it may be for the quotidian demands of everyday existence.

The tale of the impossible . . . A house with its own soul. A death. A resurrection. A moor's pestilential environment. A house that outwardly manifests the crumbling nature of Roderick's inner decay. A febrile, fantastical story that served as an occult tale for our voices and senses to find their expression through. The actors became the house and its decaying fabric, spoke as the stones and memories of the house that are seared into its walls . . . became the death rattle and atmosphere and environment. Since humans are born of the environment they must reflect it.

59. Steven Berkoff as Roderick Usher in 1976.

60.
USHER: . . . *my walls are*
                Bleak walls, vacant eyelike windows
                set amidst a few rank sedges,
                White trunks of decayed trees.

61. Shelley Lee as Madeline Usher in the 1975 production at the Hampstead Theatre Club. Madeline, always intertwined like ivy or fungi with Usher, becomes the pen writing; a peacock feather will do for the quill.

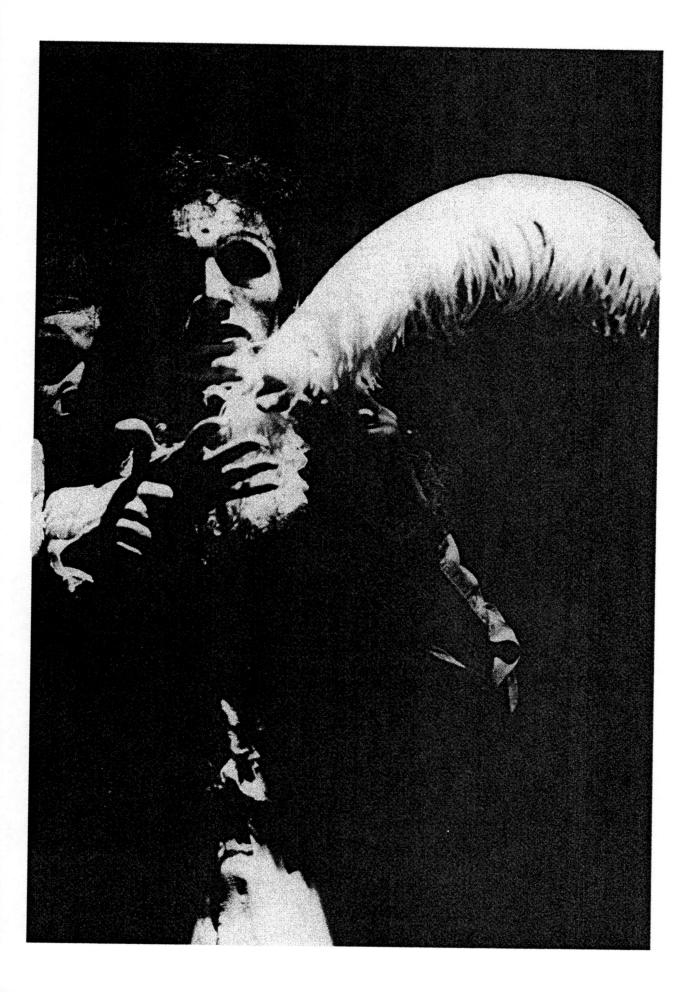

62–65. Madeline Usher spending long hours combing her hair in mime.

MADELINE: *Dark . . . The Clouds hang oppressively low . . . Is your friend coming?*

66. Terry McGinity as Usher's Friend sits and rests for a
moment after his long journey. Usher, becoming parts of the
house, conveniently 'creates' a seat for him. Opposite he
'creates' corridor and stairs.

67.
FRIEND: *Conducted in silence / Through dark and intricate /*
Passages. Everything I encounter / In this house /
Heightens vague sentiments of / Foreboding . . .

68. Terry McGinity, now as the Servant, opens the large French windows. The gust of wind hurls us back as we search the moors for signs of our Friend, our voices attempting to create the sound of the wind.

69 & 70 (*above and following two pages*). Madeline enshrouds herself in a silken fabric, a winding sheet and soft cocoon.

MADELINE: *Do you regard me with dread?*
USHER: *With astonishment.*

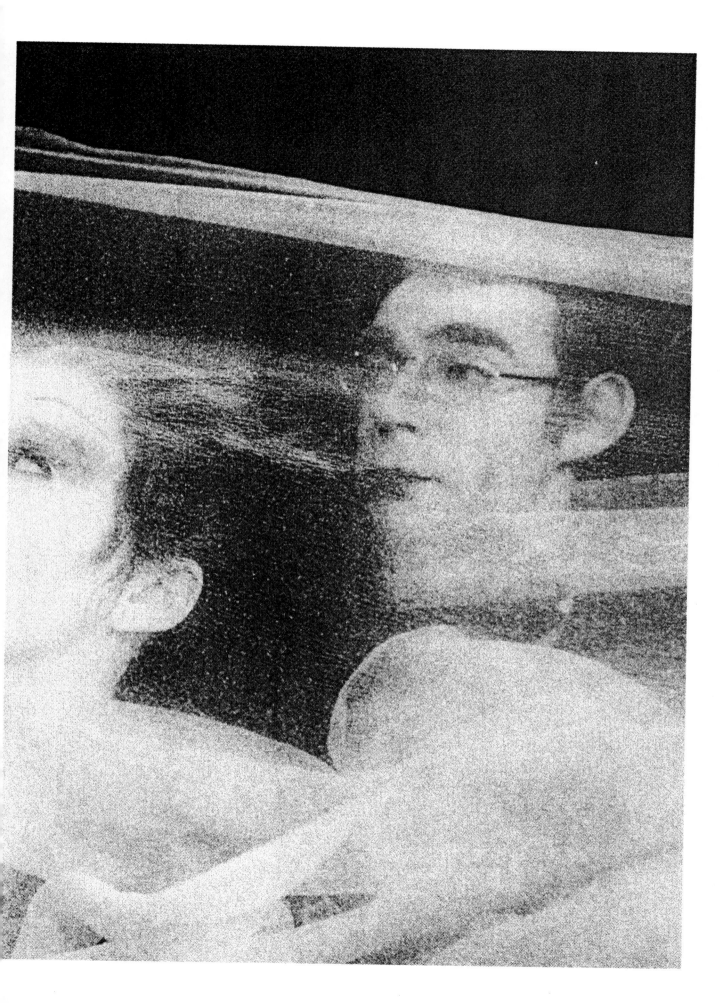

71. Eight years later Madeline Usher as metamorphosed into the skilled mime/dancer Annie Stainer for the 1982 Australian tour.

MADELINE: *He regards me with astonishment. What do you see?*

USHER: *A tenderly beloved sister.*

72. Meanwhile I, as Usher, show definite signs of decay and dementia. The years of Usher have taken their toll. Not a healthy role to act for too long.

USHER: *Catalepsy, dread wasting, disease.*

73 (*previous two pages*). The Doctor examines Madeline's stiff body that is locked in catatonia.

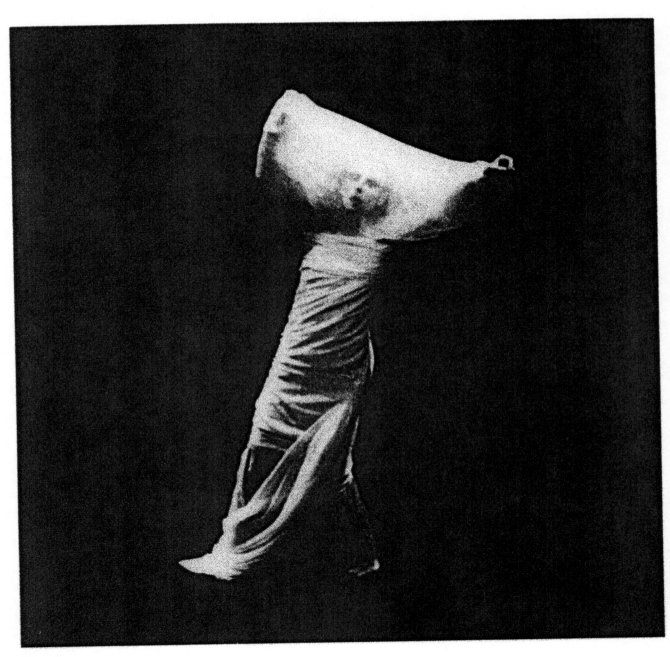

74.

USHER: *She approaches the end of her days. Her passing*
will leave me so helpless and frail.
The last of the ancient race of the Ushers.

75.
USHER: *A gradual wasting away of the person.*
Frequent though transient affections of a partially
cataleptical nature.

Agamemnon is about energy of a different kind, but overlaps with my play *East*. It is filtered through my own impression of Greece and is rooted more in the elements of landscape and sea . . . It is also about heat and battle, fatigue, the marathon and the obscenity of modern and future wars. Naturally it is about the body and its pleasures and pains. I followed Aeschylus but chose to take my own route from time to time. Events smudge into each other and I have used from the Feast of Atreus the ghastly origins of the curse. This is a suitable horrific beginning, though horror was not what I wanted but a revelation of the crime. I described it as if it had happened to me.

The final text evolved after a long workshop series during which the actors turned themselves into athletes, soldiers, horses and chorus. The text was chanted, spoken, sung, and simply acted. I am really grateful to two actors (Wolf Kahler and Barry Philips) who started the first day (sometime in April 1973) and finished with me on the 21st August 1976. They had been through each reworking and performance and gave to the production totally selfless commitment and energy. David Toop and Paul Burwell created the music and welded themselves into the action like a cunning embroidery, constantly stimulating and inspiring. And Deborah Norton gave her electrifying voice and presence to Clytemnestra.

In 1984 I had the opportunity to stage the play one more time in Los Angeles for the Olympic Arts Festival. The thematic coincidence was a happy one. What better play than *Agamemnon*? I suggested the idea of working with black actors to my producer and we auditioned most of the non-white actors in Los Angeles. I am ready to plead guilty to any charges that may be laid, in that I was looking for athleticism, fervour, community spirit for the Chorus and strong voices. They had all of these qualities in 'spades' and it was one of the most enjoyable experiences of my directing life.

AGAMEMNON

76. Hilton McRae being trapped as Paris in the 1976 Greenwich Theatre production.

77. The actors become a troop of horses, thundering their way back to Argos victoriously (although historically probably most inaccurately). Even though masked, one recognises Barry Philips' centred, strong and graceful movement on the right. Hilton McRae impressively leads the charge.

78. Why not make a grotesque throne out of bodies if other materials are scarce? Many long hours were spent knitting sailors' string vests together into 'chain mail'. During the Round House performances in 1973 we experimented with 'effects' of all kinds.

79. Joa L'Avila **(far left)** always compelling to watch as the Chorus.

80. Barry Philips **(left)** as the Herald.

81. Berkoff **(bottom left)** as Agamemnon.

82. Forever searching, experimenting and just hitting on another way to suggest the waves of the storm-dashed sea, the cast reconfigures a rope into a ship being lashed about.

CHORUS: *The seas like waves of great iced claws / The colour of phlegm / stern hawsers hold us fast or we'd be mashed by them.*

83 & 84 *(left and bottom left)*. The Trojans and Greeks locked in mortal combat.

CHORUS: *Javelins a splinter / Knees hit the dust /
Trojans drowning in each other's blood /
Bones shattered at first clash / Mouths turn to
rust.*

85 *(below)*. Poles were a useful way of binding the Chorus and the battle together and pointing the language into one seamless fusion of word and action.

CHORUS: *Javelin / arrow / spear / sword / axe /
cut / thrust / tear / bleed / hack!*

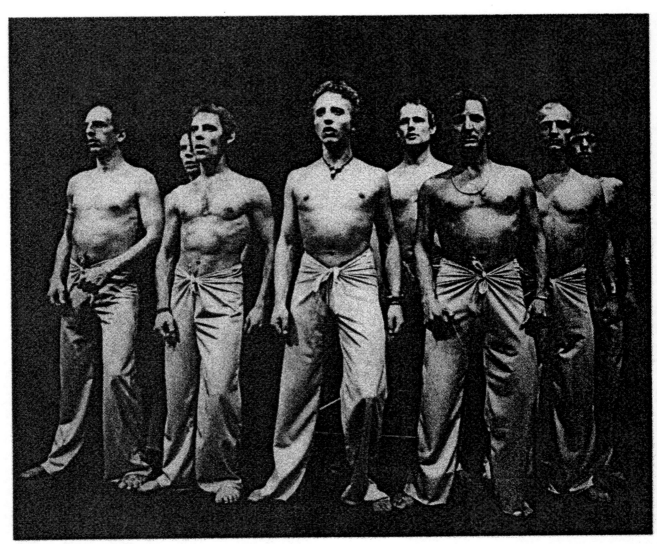

86. A second version of the play at the Greenwich Theatre in 1976 where simple cotton pants have replaced string vests. The Chorus has a cleaner, neutral look that is more classical in line.

CHORUS: *Ten years since Agamemnon and Menelaus*
Twin bronze fists of the House of Atreus . . .

87. Berkoff as Agamemnon again – a touch of 'Che' here – as I tried everything for a look, even a pair of NHS specs.

88. Deborah Norton as Clytemnestra. Her splendid voice rang through the theatre.

CLYTEMNESTRA: *Fire travels / Fire speaks / The God of fire raced from peak to peak / The God of fire leapt / scorched crackles and shrieks . . .*

89. Ten years of battle and at last Agamemnon returns home.

AGAMEMNON: *First I hail Argos and her Gods who know the right course from the wrong . . .*

90. Clytemnestra. Deborah Norton's stony face says it all.

CHORUS: *Agamemnon murdered his own child . . . /*
Clytemnestra vows to avenge the bloody deed /
and on it goes / without an end / the curse first
laid on the House of Atreus.

91 & 92. Hilton McRae as Paris
gets his just desserts.

93 & 94. Battle scenes of Trojan versus Greek,
performed this time as in a classical frieze.
The dance-like battle took twenty minutes to execute.

95. Wolf Kahler as the Watchman
reports the fatal triumph.

WATCHMAN: *Shout out the news to Agamemnon's queen /*
Troy is fallen / Awake and sing!

96. In 1979 I had the opportunity to stage the play in Israel. Here there was a sense of solidarity and identity with the scenes of conflict. The Hebrew language sounded quite natural and highly dramatic and powerful.

97. Whereas I once created a sea kinetically out of tightly stretched rope, now I experimented with bodies which in the end I preferred.

98. Soldiers in battle. We dressed the actors this time as padded American football players to stress athleticism and power. The stage was marked off as a square, the battle likened to a game or contest.

99. *'Screaming like eagles / maddened for the prey /*

101. *their nest pillaged / clawed hate /*

100. *wings beating, they swooped / they ripped and tore /*

102. *the gods above heard the furore . . .'*

103. Asher SarFaty as Agamemnon struts while his serpentine wife, ably played by Joanna Peled, tries to 'crawl' round him. Peled was an ex-'La Mama' actress and played Clytemnestra with a mixture of New York and Israeli panache.

104. For Clytemnestra's costume I took Oskar Schlemmer's Bauhaus idea of a garment inspired by the movement of the body. But there are also some resemblances to a tall lampshade.

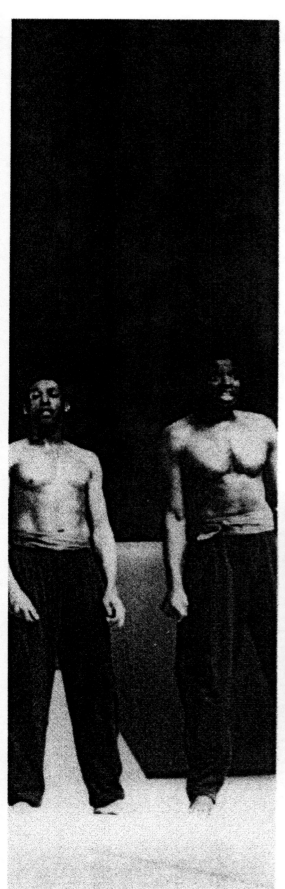

105. Roger Guenveur Smith running as the Herald to impart the news of Troy's surrender and decimation. It was an energetic performance equal to that of Barry Philips who created the original role and who helped on this all-black production at the 1984 Olympic Arts Festival in Los Angeles.

106.

CHORUS: *Two leaders, one in thought, with a forest of spears / in thousands pointing north / scented the distant blood of Troy.*

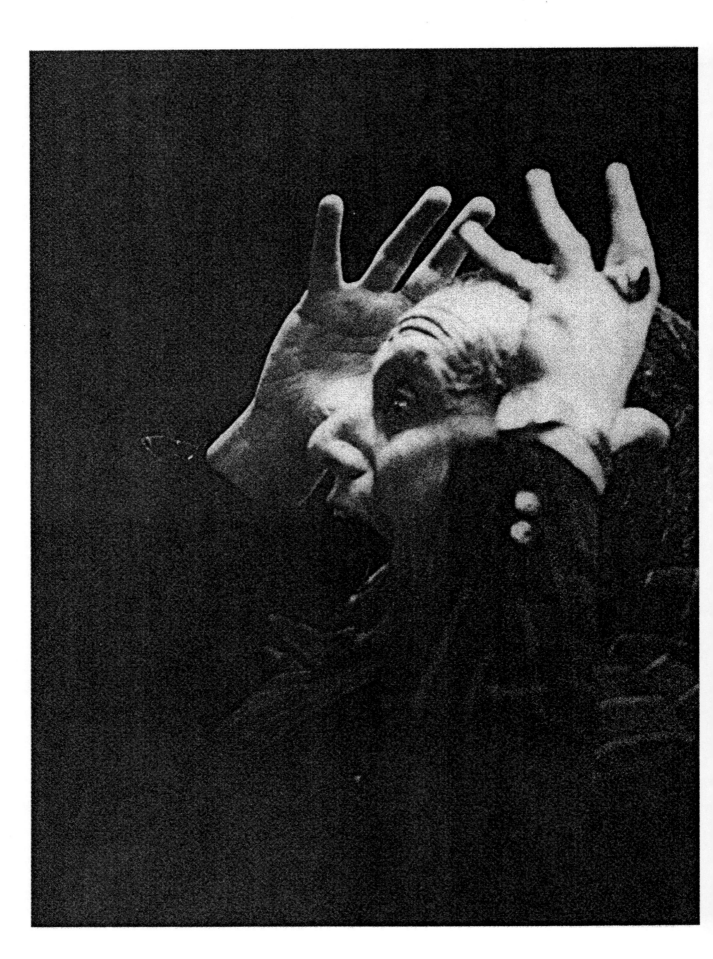

In every actor is a Hamlet struggling to get out. In fact, in most directors too. For whatever reason, and there are many, Hamlet is the accumulation of all our values and beliefs. In him are set out the rules for the perfect human, the perfect rationalist, plus the adventurer, all rolled into one. No other play gives an actor such words of compassion, charm, wisdom, wit, moral force, insight and philosophy.

The actor needs to feel those things within his own breast and to touch these words is to set alight a small flame within himself. We all wish to be . . . Hamlet, and cast our torch over the iniquities and sins of others as he does now and will do in the future, and in all times and in all styles.

Hamlet is a feast for the actor since there is something naturally of Hamlet in us all . . . There is maybe one speech that will touch one actor more than another, one scene that fits so like a glove while another does not. Since Hamlet touches the complete alphabet of human experience every actor feels he is born to play him. The bold extrovert will dazzle and play with the word power, the scenes of vengeance, and blast Ophelia and Gertrude off the stage. The introvert will see every line pointed at him, the outsider, the loner, the watcher, he, with his one trusting friend, and a quick answer for everything lest it be a barb. The wit will play for laughs and the lunatic for madness. The romantic for ideals. So you cannot be miscast for Hamlet — '*fatally* miscast' as one critic called me in fact — since he too had *his* version of Hamlet fixed in his head. I chose Hamlet and staged it with utter simplicity as if we were dissecting the play under the lights of an operating theatre. Although I functioned as an actor it was a director's concept.

107. Berkoff as Hamlet
first sees the Ghost of his father.
The 1980 Round House production.

108. The 'family' photo call. Our group of actors toured Europe during 1981–82. The cast came and went over the three years that we spent performing *Hamlet*, but the three in front, Matthew Scurfield, Linda Marlowe and me, remained in the cast throughout.

109. Wolf Kahler ominously leads me on.

GHOST: *'Tis given out that sleeping in my orchard*
         A serpent stung me . . .

110.
POLONIUS: *What do you read my lord?*
HAMLET: *Words, words, words.*

111. Anything for a laugh? . . . or a serious attempt at 'acting' mad.

HAMLET: *. . . for yourself, sir, shall grow old as I am, if like a crab, you could go backwards.*
POLONIUS: *[Aside] Though this be madness, yet there is method in 't.*

112. Matthew Scurfield gloating as Claudius.

CLAUDIUS: *If he by chance escape your venom'd stuck,*
                        Our purpose may hold there.

113.
HAMLET: *Now might I do it pat, now 'a is a-praying;*
                  And now I'll do 't. And so 'a goes to heaven,
                  And so am I revenged.

114. I staged the killing of Claudius in my mind's eye inspired by some music by John Prior. I first 'kill' the king in mime as wish fulfilment. But then we reversed the whole action like a reel of film and I find I cannot do it 'for real'.

115. The closet scene with Linda Marlowe as Gertrude.

GERTRUDE: *Whereon do you look?*
HAMLET: *On him, on him! Look you how pale he glares.*

116.
HAMLET: *Look here, upon this picture, and on the
counterfeit presentment of two brothers.*

117.
HAMLET: *Here is your husband like a mildewed
ear blasting his wholesome brother.*

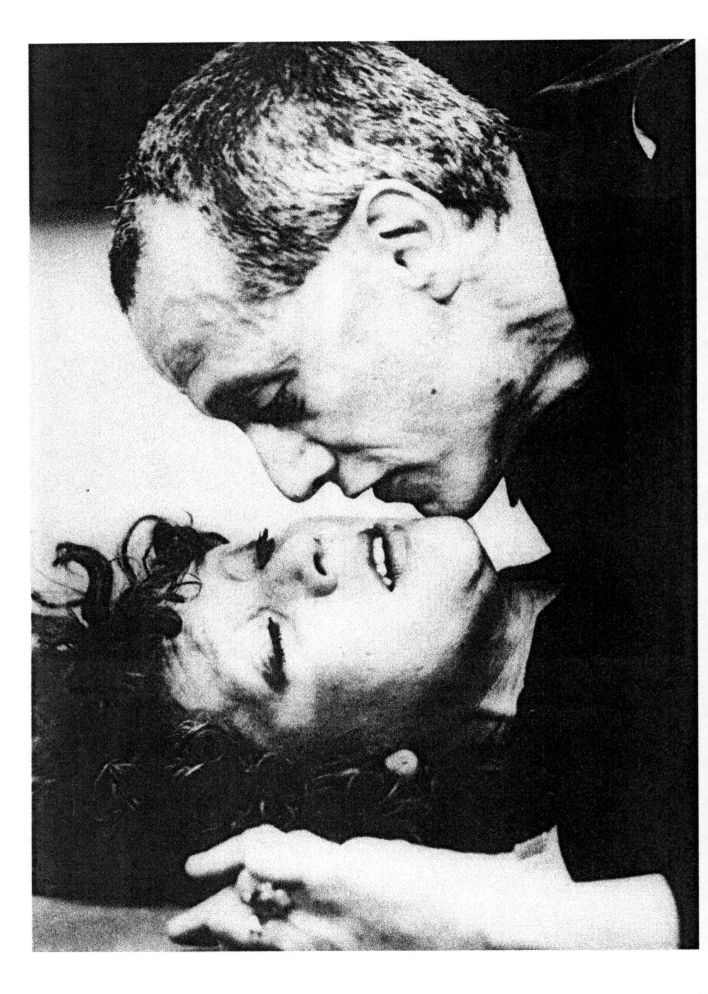

118. One of Roger Morton's best photographs. It captures the erotic tension between Hamlet and Gertrude in this most intimate of scenes.

HAMLET: *Oh 'tis sweet when in one line two crafts directly meet.*

119. HAMLET: *My fate cries out . . . Unhand me, gentlemen.*

120. Laertes, played by Barry Philips, and I fight over the body of Ophelia. As elsewhere, I seem to like bodies fighting against obstacles. Restriction affords the actor interesting positions.

121 & 122. Claudius receives his just desserts as I, with an imaginary sword, thrust home. Matthew Scurfield, however, really made you believe it hit its mark.

CORIOLANUS

This was my second Shakespeare production after *Hamlet* and I enjoyed creating it just as much. This time I did not have the arduous task of creating and playing the title role.

I liked the sinuous text and the conflict between opposing forces which occurs throughout the play: Plebeians versus Autocrat, State versus Individual, Aufidius versus Coriolanus, Mother versus Son. It was an interesting experiment, dressed in modern with overtones of the fascist state, and well suited to the American actors who, to a man, were excellent in the roles. They gave Shakespeare a fresh and contemporary slant. Christopher Walken was a 'gangster' Coriolanus, effective and chilling, while the renowned Irene Worth played Volumnia for a third time and with her usual steely vocal power. Elements of this production were then duplicated in Munich in 1991.

Some of the techniques of *Hamlet* I borrowed for *Coriolanus*. Like most directors I feed upon myself for ideas. But the idea for the Chorus that is central to the play and the ensemble acting that resulted was influenced by New York street life.

123. Irene Worth as Volumnia, Keith David as Aufidius and Christopher Walken as Coriolanus at Joseph Papp's New York Public Theatre in 1989.

124 (below). Coriolanus plus Troops ride into battle as Coriolanus dreams of conquering Aufidius. The Chorus was a multi-purpose group of actors, going from plebeians to soldiers to onlookers, thus developing a strong unity of style through movement and becoming in the end a formidable ensemble.

125 (top right). Coriolanus reprimands his Troops with a powerful slap.

126 (middle right). The Troops are pleased to see him.

127 (bottom right). Aufidius celebrates in his tent. Coriolanus watches from the outside . . . always the outsider.

128. Here the chaps are the 'Aufidius team' and bear a striking resemblance to Sicilian mafiosi. We all visited a second-hand clothes store off Broadway and squeezed into jackets that were too tight and then ripped them. The chairs were the only elements of 'set' and were multi-functional like the Chorus, who were as tightly disciplined as a dance group. They became in the end one of the stars of the play and were reviewed as such. Joe Papp, the New York producer, encouraged me along the way. The extraordinary music by Larry Spivac, who was always experimenting and trying new sounds, captured and enhanced the action, making the play live.

129. The Chorus of Citizens at the Munich
Prinzregentheater 1991.

FIRST CITIZEN: *Before we proceed any further, hear me
                speak.*
ALL: *Speak, speak.*

FIRST CITIZEN: *You are all resolved rather to die than to*
                 famish?
ALL: *Resolved, resolved.*

130.

CORIOLANUS: *You common cry of curs, whose breath I*
hate
As reek o' th' rotten fens, whose love I prize
As the dead carcasses of unburied men
That do corrupt my air, I banish you.

131. Rufus Beck as our Coriolanus in Munich.

What's the matter you dissentious rogues
That rubbing the poor itch of your opinion.
Make yourselves scabs?

East takes place within my personal memory and experience and is less a biographical text than an outburst of revolt against the sloth of my youth and a desire to turn a welter of undirected passion and frustration into a positive form. I wanted to liberate that time squandered and sometimes enjoyed into a testament to youth and energy. It is a scream or a shout of pain. It is revolt. There is no holding back or reserve in the east end of youth as I remember . . . you lived for the moment and vitally held it . . . you said what you thought and did what you felt. If something bothered you, you let it out as strongly as you could, as if the outburst could curse and therefore purge whatever it was that caused it.

One strutted and posed down the Lyceum Strand, the Mecca of our world, performed a series of rituals that let people know who and what you were, and you would fight to the death to defend that particular lifestyle that was your own. East could be the east side of any city where the unveneered blast off at each other in their own compounded argot as if the ordinary language of polite communication was as dead as the people who uttered it.

I stylized events further by some cross-fertilization with Shakespeare and threw in a few classical allusions – this seemed to help take it out further into a ritual and yet defined it with a distinct edge. I experimented in verse and found a flow of verbal imagery the origin of which I could not readily understand. It was as if the structure inspired great freedom. A kind of flowing blank verse streamed forth. It was liberating to play and for the audience to see.

EAST

132. The 1976 Greenwich Theatre production that featured (*left to right*) Matthew Scurfield as Dad, Barry Philips as Les, Anna Nygh as Sylv, and Berkoff as Mike.

133.
LES: *Donate a snout, Mike?*

134.
LES: *My pure and angel face, my blessed boat did, on that sacred night receive his homage . . . red did flow.*

135.
LES: *Oh! Ho! I gushed. You fancied me around the back with boots and chains and knives . . .*

136.
MIKE: *OK. I'll bung thee a snout.*

137.
MIKE: *So I said to him 'fuck off thou discharge from thy mother's womb before with honed and sweetened razor I do trouble to remove thy balls from thee.'*

138.
MIKE: *So what if sly old Sylv had led me on a touch by showing out to all the lads, provoking hard-ons and gang wars between opposing tribes . . .*

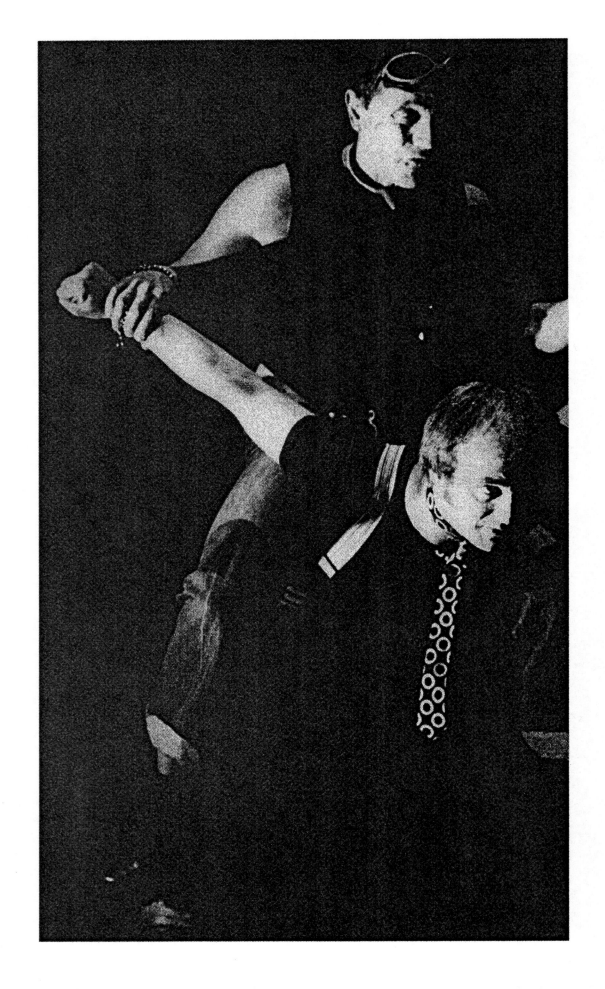

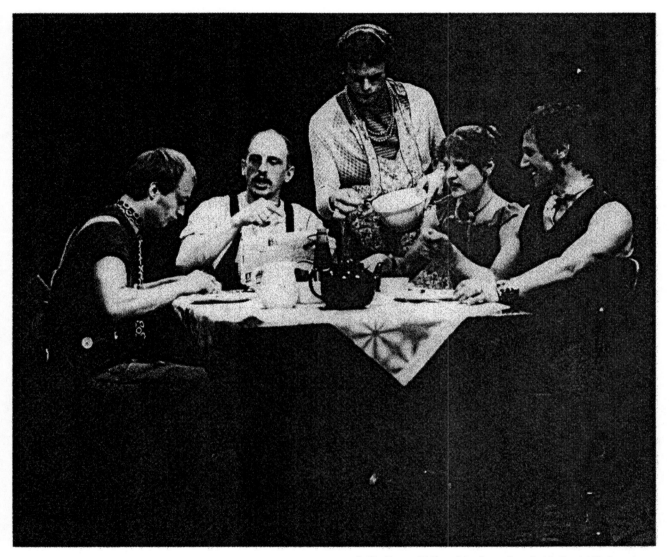

140. Barry Philips, Matthew Scurfield, David Delve, Anna Nygh and Me.

DAD: *You don't want to believe all that rubbish about detector vans. That's just to scare you . . .*

139. Barry Philips and I create our own fantasy motorbike — much better than a real one even though Barry's exhaust pipe could do with a service!

141. The Lads chat up Sylv.

MIKE: *She became with me a fun-palace in which almighty raging technicolour and panoramic skin-flicks would be enacted.*

142–145. Anna Nygh's curvacious, well-trained and articulate body ran through every expression in the rending of her speech.

SYLV: *I for once would like to be a fella, unwholesome both in deed and word . . .*

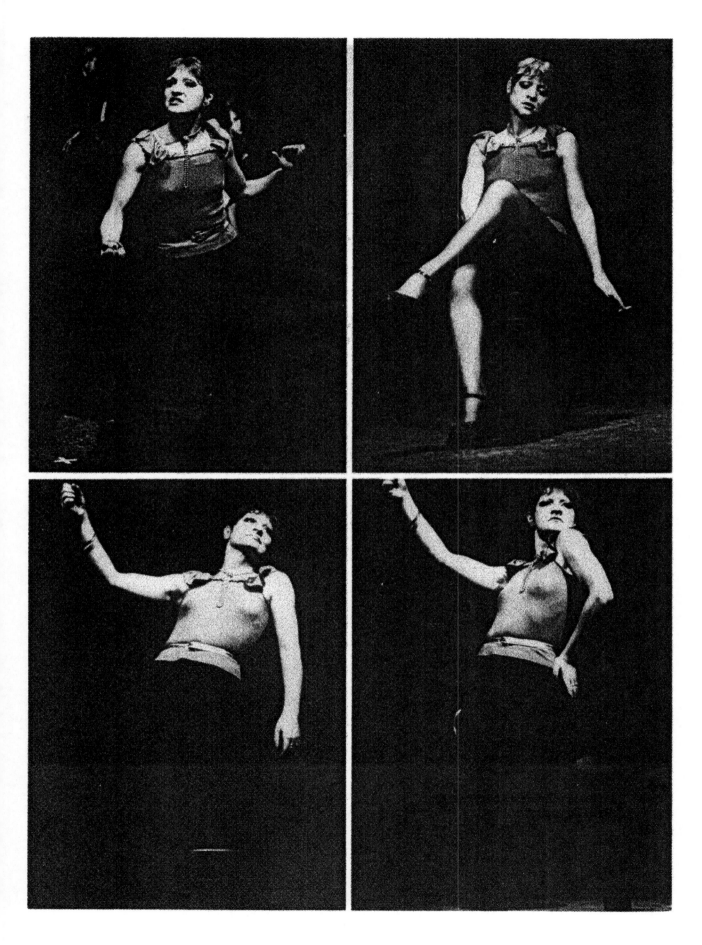

146.
MIKE: *I fancy going down the Lyceum tonight.*
           I double fancy that.

147.
MIKE: *She were in ingredients of flesh-*
pack suavely fresh . . . seam
running up the back of her leg
as if pointing the way to tourists.

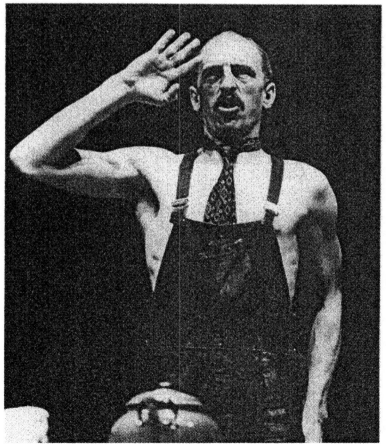

148.
DAD: *Ozzie had the right idea — put*
them in uniforms — into the
brown shirts — gave people an
identity.

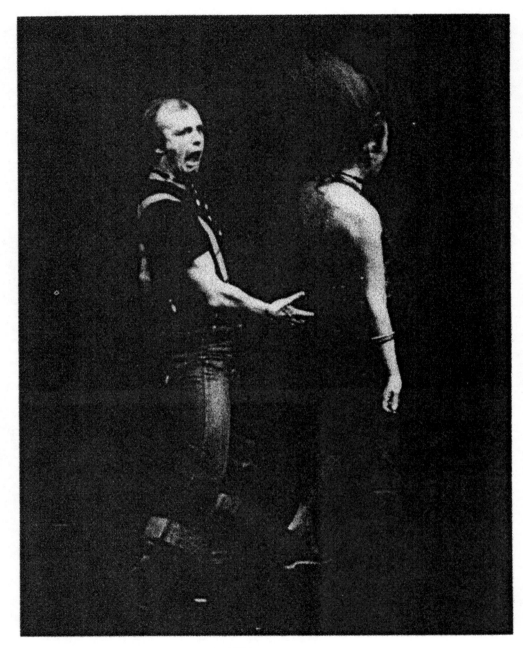

149. The cast of the Australian tour in 1978.

SYLV: *He's lying in bed while I'm on the underground, getting goosed in the rush hour between Mile End and Tottenham Court Road.*

150. Our new Sylv, ably played by Sylvia Mason, puts up with the 'Three Stooges' on our great Australian tour. She had much fortitude. Here we are photographed by Robert McFarlane, who became a good friend.

151 (*below*).
SYLV: *Piss off, thou lump – thou hast no style for me.*

152 & 153 (*above and right*). Now the extraordinary Roy McCarthy joins us as Mum and is no less wonderful than Robert Longden. There is something special about photos taken during a performance. They isolate a drama you could never capture in any other way. We did sixteen weeks in 'Oz' and loved the country. The other chaps wanted to emigrate.

Greek was my love poem to the spirit of Oedipus over the centuries. I ransacked the entire legend. So this is not simply an adaptation of Sophocles but a recreation of the various Oedipus myths which seemed to apply, particularly to a play about what I saw London had become. London equals Thebes and is full of riots, filth, decay, bombings, football mania, mobs at the palace gates, plague madness and post-pub depression.

The play dealt with the idea of an emotional, social plague – apart from the actual biological one – that I saw was eating away at the heart of this nation. It was staged simply in the usual stripped-down style I would, for want of a better term, call functionalist. The actors' white faces were like masks of Greek statues. The table became a stage in itself and the family the Greek Chorus for each other and also playing all the roles. Barry Philips played the Eddy/Oedipus role and did it with brilliant, laconic humour. Matthew Scurfield's Dad was a *tour de force* of the first order, while Linda Marlowe played Jocasta/Wife as perfectly as I would dare hope, giving the lines full meaning and emotion.

Greek came to me via Sophocles, trickling its way down the millennia until it reached the unimaginative wastelands of Tufnell Park – a land more fantasized than real, an amalgam of the deadening war zones that some areas of London have become. It was also a love story.

GREEK

154. Deirdre Morris in good form as the Sphinx.

155. Linda Marlowe recounts the horrors of the plague as the Chorus expresses the deformities that modern life brings in its wake. Good facial acting there.

WIFE: *The plague is not quite over yet, there's still a plague around the city that will not go away, but continues to rot inside the wholesome body of our state. People are dropping like flies, armed killers snipe from the shattered eyes of buildings . . . meanwhile men in white masks are penetrating the holy crucible where life may have slipped in, and armed with scalpels and suction pumps tear out the living fruit and sluice it down the river of sewage . . .*

156.
DAD: *The heat waves turn it all to slime and filthy germs hang thickly in the air / the rats are on the march.*

157. Deirdre Morris as Mum with ear cocked to received Dad's propaganda.

159 (above).
MUM: *More tea love?*

160 (right).
DAD: *What do you make of it son? You
            don't fancy your old mum do you
            son? You don't want to kill me do
            you boy?*

158 (*left*). Dad and Eddy fight with words, proving the axiom that words can kill: *'Hit, hurt, crunch, pain, stab, jab.'*

161. The Hoxton gang with their leader 'Curly', loosely based on a charismatic London gangster called 'Curly' King. They appear leaning against a lamp-post, each facing out like gargoyles.

CURLY: *Night and silence / that's what it's all about . . .*

West is about courage: the courage to live according to your spirit and not by the guidelines laid down for you by others; to be true to yourself, which may involve alienating others, but which you know is worth pursuing since it defines who you are. Courage shapes, forges and hones you into something that is not vague but clear-cut and definite. Mike's truth is to live for the simple principles and to put his courage where his mouth is. He defeats the Hoxton monster and will continue to fight monsters so that others can rest safe in their beds.

While the play is an allegory about demons we must defeat, it is also about an area of time and space called London and, specifically, Stamford Hill or Hackney, N16. You wore tailored suits and strutted your gear at the Lyceum, Strand, on Sunday nights. Movements were short, percussive and cool. Ted Heath led the band, Lita Rosa sang and the Kray twins would stand and survey their domain. I never saw them dance. Stamford Hill stood at the crossroads of Tottenham, Dalston and Hoxton and was subject to attacking forays from many directions. So here again London becomes transformed into epic terrain.

West was first performed at the Donmar Warehouse, Covent Garden, in May 1983. That was its world premiere, although I believe a version was performed in Wagga Wagga, Australia, three years before, in 1980. But they tampered with the text and even included a scene from East, thus disqualifying themselves from being the first to present West. East, my play about the East End from a young Hero's point of view, was the first of a series which naturally inspired West. The BBC actually commissioned it and then found it was not quite dull enough for television – so I was then able to stage it for the theatre. Limehouse Productions and Ian Albery sponsored its first showing in London, and then Limehouse filmed it for Channel 4.

WEST

162. The Hoxton gang as they strut around their
'manor'. They uttered a yob patois that was an
amalgam of curses, threats and gestures of a
confrontational kind. This was all rendered like a song
and dance and is impossible to write down in any sort
of coherent notation. (*Left to right*) Ken Sharrock,
Bruce Payne, Ralph Brown and Steve Dixon.

163. Mike, played by Rory Edwards, shaping up for
the main event.

164. Sylv, played by the stunning Susan Kyd, getting prepared for the night's activities.

SYLV: *It was November / the last dead leaves of Autumn / were falling off the perch . . .*

165. The lads take an attacking stance: *'Smash, splatter, punch, kick, nut!'*

DECADENCE

Decadence is a study of the ruling classes or upper classes, so called by virtue of the strangulated vowel tones rather than any real achievement. The voice is caught in the back of the throat and squashed so as to release as little emotion as possible. Consonants are hard and biting, since emotion is carried on the vowel. The upper class slur the vowel or produce a glottal stop, which by closing down of the glottis creates an impure vowel – as in 'hice' for 'house'. They move in awkward rapid gestures or quick jerks and sometimes speak at rapid speeds to avoid appearing to have any feeling for what they say. They achieve pleasure very often in direct relation to the pain they cause in achieving it. Particularly in causing intolerable suffering to achieve exquisite pâtés, boiling lobsters alive with other crustaceans and hunting down defenceless animals to give them (the hunters) a sense of purpose on Sundays.

Creating the play was a desire to let loose the fantasies that inspired unbridled indulgence. Of course the protagonists would have to be super well-heeled, upper-class toffs since they are so easy a target of satire. But no less risible were the working class yobbos who set out to dethrone them. It was less a battle of classes than a series of sketches about greed and jealousy. It was very good for the play since upper-class types are already such parodies of human nature – but then, so are the extremes of the working classes.

166. Linda Marlowe as Helen gives Steve, Steven Berkoff, a few hints on the finer points of fox hunting.

167. The sofa was the one piece of set and furniture. Everything else in the way of props was mimed with exquisite finesse. STEVE: *We escaped to the restaurant – at last some repose.*

Linda Marlowe patiently listening to Steve's waffle.

168 & 169.

STEVE: More champagne! It showers away the fish and the garlic / the slightly acid taste / the burp, the sliver of nausea that starts to grow / from compound of prawns, salmon, beef, oysters, the sparkly flows . . .

170. Here the character of Les tries to impersonate a rat, the outstretched hands describing the width of the whiskers.

171.
LES: *All safe he thinks and opens up / a ten inch blade drives in his gut.*

172. Henry Goodman, Berkoff, Anita Dobson and Thelma Ruby in the 1991 London production.

173. The kvetching continues in the side frames.

The play was first staged in California in front of a large painted wall depicting the freeways of Los Angeles as a surreal multi-laned jam of cars. There must have been about twenty lanes and one saw them all converge in the distance. Half-way up the wall was an impervious blue sky. Downstage was a table and four chairs around which the actors performed.

The movement was generally sharp and dynamic. The declarations to the audience meant as confessions and given their full value. When a character was speaking his or her thoughts the action was frozen in the last position they were in and held for the duration, almost like a freeze-frame . . . Scenes would flow easily into each other much as a dissolve in a film.

The London production finally opened in the autumn of 1991 and was our English version of *Kvetch*. The painted wall of freeways became instead a big window out of which Frank considers jumping. The play is a study of the effects of anxiety on the nagging kvetch that keeps you awake and drives you crazy. It is the demon that wishes to taste your blood and sucks your confidence.

KVETCH

174. So much of the acting in this play is done by the face.

'Stress comes in many different forms . . .'

175. Stanley Lebor joins the group for the second half.

'We all live under the shadow of the bomb – cancer – carcinogens – illness – unemployment – impotence – fear of fear – blacks – whites – police – rates – income tax – forgetting our lines . . .'

SINK THE BELGRANO

Sink the Belgrano was my anti-war statement when Britain sent troops into the Falklands. Like most people I was amazed at the outbreak of hostilities. As we drew into the twilight years of this bloody century, we had to have a reprise of the Second World War, with all the attendant war cries and news coverage as if we were fighting the Hun all over again.

When the battleship General Belgrano was sunk with its terrible loss of life, the Argentines retaliated, leading to an even more horrific loss of life. A gruesome waste. Several years after the event I met Desmond Rice who, with Arthur Gavshon, had written a book on the incident which then inspired me to write my play. I wrote much of it in verse to distance it and free it from the kind of 'ageing' that contemporary plays suffer from and to attempt to give it a universal tone. I borrowed the patriotic fervour that flavours Shakespeare's *Henry V*, and tried to capture the 'war' mood that gripped the whole of Britain. It was the first and only play I've written to be based on actual contemporary events. I was blessed with a first-class crew and was proud of the production. Unfortunately, like the Belgrano, it was badly torpedoed and attacked by some hostile reviews but survived a respectable run at the Half Moon Theatre and then transferred to London's Mermaid Theatre.

176. 'Maggie' played at the Mermaid Theatre in 1986 by Louise Gold after the role was created at the Half Moon Theatre by Maggie Steed. Tam Dean Burn (*left*) and Eugene Lipinski (*right*) gaze up at Maggot with the devotion of children.

177. Tam Dean Burn, Richard Earthy and Eugene Lipinski (*left to right*) show completely individual reactions as the Belgrano is hit by a torpedo. Their faces capture the mixed reaction to the news.

CHORUS: *Dead men were*
                 everywhere in bits.
            A piece of arm and here
                 a leg
            Upon the deck a figure
                 covered in burning oil
            Three hundred and thirty
                 sailors died at once.

178. Rory Edwards as Chorus harangues the chaps to rise and wake-up.

179. Tam Dean Burn, Eugene Lipinski, Richard Earthy, Terry McGinity (Commander), George Dillon.

CHORUS: *Oh you most brave and valiant Englishmen*
Who never shall, no never bear the yoke
Of shame or curdled pride beneath the boot
Of some o'erweening greasy foreign bloke.
We smashed the damned Spanish might . . .
We put the Hun upon the British rack,
The Boers we kicked to kingdom come
And now the Argies sneaked behind our back.

SALOME

According to Oscar Wilde's maxim life copies art. So it was fascinating to witness on an afternoon in Paris a group of street artists using their bodies in a way I had seldom seen used. They were moving very slowly to the music and impersonating those slow-motion shoot-outs one sees in Hollywood westerns when the bad guy bites the dust ultra-slow and the blood spurts. The control of their bodies was nothing short of masterly. An utterly disciplined team moving like creatures from another planet, almost weightless in the hot afternoon of the Pompidou Centre where you are encouraged to display your art without fear of being curtailed or censored. While I had worked before with such effects in my production of *The Trial*, I had not before considered it for a whole production. I decided the weight of Wilde's language had to be carried slowly as if it were a fragile and precious cargo capable of being shattered by anything less than the most careful handling. So I decided to try fusing this movement with the text. It seemed to marry, and the bonding was music, played delicately on a piano.

So I had to find the right style to match Oscar's style, to be a medium for his bejewelled text, and to find the right structure to allow the story to breathe with as little change as possible. So much was the perfume and tapestry in the language that I decided that the stage should be bare and allow the words to bounce off the hard surfaces without being softened or cushioned by 'carpets and ivory tables and the tables of jasper'. These are words that Wilde liked to use but woe betide a designer who seeks to make a table of jasper. Denuded of everything but what was most vital, and so no wine bottles or glasses, nothing that we could not control or change, nothing whose physical laws were subject to gravity, accident or wilfulness. We would merely act the ingredients of the wine and the fruit so the actors would become language itself.

180. Herod attempts to woo Salome away from her desire for the Baptist's head by offering every jewel and bauble he can summon up. Katherine Schlesinger as Salome is mightily unimpressed.

181 (*previous two pages*). Herod addresses his court as they offer him 'a light'.

HEROD: *It is ridiculous to kill oneself.*

182. Carmen Du Sautoy as Herodias looks a trifle jaded as she listens to Herod's posturing.

HEROD: *Caesar is wonderful. He can do everything . . .*

183. The Chorus was like a multi-headed beast, a dance group, a party who mirrored Herod's shifting moods. A marvellous ensemble of individual performers which included (*left to right*) George Dillon, Vincenzo Ricotta, Imogen Claire, Katrin Cartlidge, Tim Potter, Wolf Kahler, Maria Pastel, Jason Carter.

184 & 185 (*below*).
HEROD: *I have jewels hidden in this place . . . jewels that are marvellous to look at.*

186 (*right*).
HEROD: *I will not look at things, I will not suffer things to look at me. Put out the torches! Hide the moon! Hide the stars!*

188.
HEROD: *The moon has a strange look tonight . . .*
HERODIAS: *No; the moon is like the moon, that is all.*

187.
HEROD: *O Salome, Salome, dance for me!*

189.
HEROD: *Who has taken my ring? There was a ring on my
         right hand. Who has drunk my wine? There was
         wine in my cup. It was full of wine. Someone has
         drunk it!*

190 (right). Steven Berkoff 1989.

Text Acknowledgements

The author and publisher wish to thank the following publishers for permission to quote from Introductions and excerpts that appear in the following plays and books by Steven Berkoff:

Metamorphosis, The Trial, In the Penal Colony
(Amber Lane Press)

The Fall of the House of Usher, Agamemnon
(Amber Lane Press)

Decadence, East, West, Greek
(Faber and Faber Ltd)

West and Other Plays (including *Harry's Christmas* and *Lunch*)
(Faber and Faber Ltd)

Kvetch and *Acapulco*
(Faber and Faber Ltd)

Sink the Belgrano and *Massage*
(Faber and Faber Ltd)

Salome
(Faber and Faber Ltd)

I Am Hamlet
(Faber and Faber Ltd)

Photograpic Credits

Jaacov Agor: 96, 97, 98, 99, 100, 101, 102, 103, 104

Lore Bermbach: 19, 20, 21, 22, 23, 51, 52, 53, 54, 55, 56, 57, 58

Christopher Casler: 105, 106

Nobby Clark: 1, 2, 74, 75, 180, 181, 182, 183, 184, 185, 186, 187, 188, 189, 190

John Haynes: 176, 177, 178, 179

Wilfried Hösl: 129, 130, 131

Neil Libbert: 37

Robert McFarlane: 71, 72, 73, 149, 150, 151, 152, 153

Roger Morton: 3, 9, 10, 11, 12, 13, 14, 15, 16, 17, 18, 36, 38, 39, 40, 41, 42, 43, 44, 45, 46, 47, 48, 49, 50, 59, 60, 61, 62, 63, 64, 65, 66, 67, 68, 69, 70, 76, 77, 78, 79, 80, 81, 82, 83, 84, 85, 86, 87, 88, 89, 90, 91, 92, 93, 94, 95, 107, 108, 109, 110, 111, 112, 113, 114, 115, 116, 117, 118, 119, 120, 121, 122, 132, 133, 134, 135, 136, 137, 138, 139, 140, 141, 142, 143, 144, 145, 146, 147, 148, 154, 155, 156, 157, 158, 159, 160

Alastair Muir: 172, 173, 174, 175

Christopher Pearce: 161, 162, 163, 164, 165, 166, 167, 168, 169, 170, 171

Robert Pederson: front cover

Martha Swope: 4, 23, 24, 25, 26, 27, 28, 29, 30, 31, 32, 33, 34, 35, 123, 124, 125, 126, 127, 128, back cover

Cordelia Weedon: 5, 6, 7, 8

Lightning Source UK Ltd.
Milton Keynes UK
03 February 2011

166833UK00002B/1/P